PAX ATOMICA

PAX
ATOMICA

poems

CAMPBELL
McGRATH

An Imprint of HarperCollins*Publishers*

HarperCollins books may be purchased for educational, business, or sales promotional use. For information please write: Special Markets Department, HarperCollins Publishers, 10 East 53rd Street, New York, NY 10022.

FIRST PAPERBACK EDITION 2005

Designed by Fearn Cutler de Vicq

The Library of Congress has catalogued the hardcover edition as follows:
McGrath, Campbell, 1962–
Pax atomica : poems / Campbell McGrath.—1st ed.
p. cm
ISBN 0-06-074564-9
1. United States—Civilization—Poetry. I. Title
PS3563.C3658P39 2004
811'.54—dc22
2004047156

ISBN-10: 0-06-075804-X ISBN-13: 978-0-06-075804-2 (pbk.)

02 03 04 05 ❖/RRD 10 9 8 7 6 5 4 3 2 1

For 1962

ACKNOWLEDGMENTS

My thanks to the editors of the following journals and anthologies in which these poems, some under different titles, originally appeared: *Chicago Review, Electronic Poetry Review, Georgia Review, Harvard Review, Mad Love, Michigan Quarterly Review, Mipoesía, The New American Poets* (Breadloaf/University Press of New England, 2001), *The New Yorker, Pleiades, Poets of the New Century* (Godine, 2002), *Power Lines: The Guild Complex Anthology* (Tia Chucha Press, 2001), *River Styx, Salmagundi, Smartish Pace, Sycamore Review, TriQuarterly, Witness.*

And my deep gratitude to Florida International University, and the John D. and Catherine T. MacArthur Foundation.

CONTENTS

PAX ATOMICA

▼

GIRL WITH BLUE PLASTIC RADIO

The first song I ever heard was "The Ballad of Bonnie and Clyde."
There was a girl at the playground with a portable radio,
lying in the grass near the swing set, beyond the sun-lustred
     aluminum slide,

kicking her bare feet in the air, her painted toenails—toes
the color of blueberries, rug burns, yellow pencils, Grecian urns.
This would be when—1966? No, later, '67 or '68. And no,

it was not the very first song I ever heard,
but the first that invaded my consciousness in that elastically joyous
way music does, the first whose lyrics I tried to learn,

my first communication from the gigawatt voice
of the culture—popular culture, mass culture, our culture—
     kaboom!—
raw voltage embraced for the sheer thrill of getting juiced.

Who wrote that song? When was it recorded, and by whom?
Melody lost in the database of the decades
but still playing somewhere in the mainframe cerebellums

of its dandelion-chained, banana-bike-riding, Kool-Aid-
addled listeners, still echoing within the flesh and blood
     mausoleums
of us, me, we, them, the self-same blades

of wind-sown crabgrass spoken of and to by Whitman,
and who could believe it would still matter
decades or centuries later, in a new millennium,

matter what we listened to, what we ate and watched, matter
that it was "rock 'n' roll," for so we knew to call it,
matter that there were hit songs, girls, TVs, fallout shelters.

Who was she, her with the embroidered blue jeans and bare feet,
toenails gilded with cryptic bursts of color?
She is archetypal, pure form, but no less believable for that.

Her chords still resonate, her artifacts have endured
so little changed as to need no archaeological translation.
She was older than me, worldly and self-assured.

She was, already, a figure of erotic fascination.
She knew the words and sang the choruses
and I ran over from the sandbox to listen

to a world she cradled in one hand, transistorized oracle,
blue plastic embodiment of our neo–Space Age ethos.
The hulls of our Apollonian rocket ships were as yet
        unbarnacled

and we still found box turtles in the tall weeds and mossy grass
by the little creek not yet become what it was all becoming
in the wake of the yellow earth-movers, that is:

suburbia. Alive, vibrant, unself-consciously evolving,
something new beneath the nuclear sun, something new in the
    acorn-scented dark.
Lived there until I was seven in a cinder block garden

apartment. My prefab haven, my little duplex ark.
And the name of our subdivision was
Americana Park.

THE HUMAN HEART

We construct it from tin and ambergris and clay,
    ochre, graph paper, a funnel
    of ghosts, whirlpool
in a downspout full of midsummer rain.

It is, for all its freedom and obstinance,
    an artifact of human agency
    in its maverick intricacy,
its chaos reflected in earthly circumstance,

its appetites mirrored by a hungry world
    like the lights of the casino
    in the coyote's eye. Old
as the odor of almonds in the hills around Solano,

filigreed and chancelled with flavor of blood oranges,
    fashioned from moonlight,
    yarn, nacre, cordite,
shaped and assembled valve by valve, flange by flange,

and finished with the carnal fire of interstellar dust.
    We build the human heart
    and lock it in its chest
and hope that what we have made can save us.

TRAIN JOURNAL

Song of the real, song of the absolute, song of the concrete.

Song of seedpods in cottony eruption.

Song of data, song of the specific, song of proper names, song of
    Rahway, song of Trenton and Philadelphia.

Song of Wilmington, Wilmington, Wilmington, Delaware.

Song of the forms and embodiments of neglect.

Song of junk.

Song of the seen, the shutter flash, binary code of the eyelids, song
    of the open and shut.

Song of the optic nerve, song of the convex, the mirrored, the
    reciprocal, song of waves, song of serial mimesis, song of
    illumination.

Song of the distribution network, the feeder pattern, circuitry, the
    grid.

Song of transitions and electrical charges, song of elements, song of
    change.

Song of FRANCO RESTAURANT RATED #1 SPAGHETTI.

Song of the hewn and hafted, of cutting and clearance, song of the
    work crew.

Song of the blind alley, song of the random roadblock, song of the
    arrow of intention.

Song of dirt, song of asphalt, song of the tracks as they parallel the
    road, song of the Walt Whitman Rest Stop.

• • • •

Theme and variation, theme and variation.
Click-clack, click-clack:
I don't *know*, I don't *know*, I don't *know*.

. . . .

Things beneath blue tarps, things beneath green tarps, buttresses
    and red mud, sense of estrangement, bafflement, loss.
Grey despairing factory buildings, the lashing out in anger.
Plow blades and safety cones heaped behind the construction shed,
    phone couplings, utility boxes of unknown denomination,
    great spools of orange cable.
A yellow sign: TANNING.
Used-car lots aglint in winter sun.
Pickup trucks and Harleys in the dirt lot of a roadhouse meadowed
    among cattails in the orphan lands.

. . . .

World sliding past
like an illuminated manuscript,

like the *Book of Kells.*

. . . .

Weak snow along the ashen verge, soot and gravel, wild sumac.
Boulevards, fast-food mansards, the Greyhound depot in ruins.
Shells of displaced meaning, crushed hulls I've seen before,

but not here.

If not here, then
where?

What other world than this?

. . . .

And these its vestments: thistle crowns, transformers
and warehouses, ink, husked reeds, trees shredded
to pulp and stewed and sheeted, this paper,
this poem, this silver train, every train in the station,
every person on the platform, their hats and gloves,
their fabric, every stitch, every thread, every syllable.

. . . .

Jimmy Joe's Roofing
89 Pacific Street
Newark, New Jersey!

. . . .

Semaphore of light and shadow as the forest closes on the tracks,
branchings and articulations like the microfolds of the self,
genie of the cerebrum,

                              dot-dash code of the trees,
solitary or undifferentiable, those that seem to speak of suffering,
others prayerful, intent on the sky—

                              too much to call them joyous?
Many that are indifferent, stunted or damaged, marsh-whitened,
shriven, voiceless.

                    At night there is no forest.

                              · · · ·

Song of the absolute
          rock bottom price guarantee.
Song of the real
          24-HOUR XXX GIRLS.
Song of the concrete
          backyard gnome.

                              · · · ·

Sense of existence as a journey on a speeding vehicle,
a space capsule veiled in the heat of re-entry,
transactional rage and afterglow,
time the blind vector angled against,

time as aura or aurora,
time as atmosphere and the body engulfed
in the fire of the passed-through,
the goddess in her nimbus of sparks and loss.

. . . .

Or are we the rocks
and it the river
flowing, coursing past?

. . . .

Song of the conjoined, song of the conjured, song of raised arms at
    the crossing, song of slabs and coiled serpents.
Song of drawn curtains, of the bespoken, song of the dimly lit by
    eventide.
Song of the reverential lightning bolt, song of the lordly upwelling.
Song of the cigarette billboard, of graffiti in the overpass, SHADEY N
    LUIS 4 EVER.
Song of the grindstone, song of the flywheel, song of the lost
    Walker Evans church on the hill.
Song of the RV and the barbed-wire school bus farm.
Song of the sapling, song of the chain saw, song of cordwood.
Song of pondwater, ditchwater, sumpwater, swampwater.
Song of Christmas lights, tangled swing chains and murals on brick,
    song of rust, song of golden pollen.

Song of CONGOLEUM.

Song of the subdivision, the suburb, the smokestack, the city.

Song of the gouged earth, the harrow, the plow, song of the
    cornfield, of geese and ducks, song of what migrates.

Song of the trashed semi-trailer, song of the corridor of
    abandonment.

Song of the danger icon, song of the flashing orb, song of the
    Jungian eyeball.

Song of the tanker, the reefer, the gondola, the box.

Song of the radio tower.

Song of the sky, of clouds, song of crows, starlings, of stars.

. . . .

Fleets of red delivery trucks,
a field of exhausted cows,
metal sheeting lost or scrapped,
sheds of shrink-wrapped lumber.

fallow meadow

fetal slumber

. . . .

How else to parse or anagrammatize it?
How else to convey a sense of the predicament?
How else to envision grace?

How else to comprehend a sidehill of snow
and stubby pines, this sewage treatment plant?

How else to explain the beautiful

shapes of music,

wheeled monochrome metal ribbons,
pearl-carved shapes,
graven Escher and Möbius shapes

like green and saffron rings!

Like the kinesis of identity.
Like a river surmounted by housing projects.
Like the bracts of gorgon flowers.

. . . .

Song of the garment mills, song of the flags of trackside laundry, the
    glimpsed life, the spangled whatever.

Song of the boathouses on the Schuylkill, their white articulate
    bulbs and sculls.
Song of the container ship, cargo and spars in the estuarine reaches,
    song of the Susquehanna.
Song of denim, of iron and vinyl, song of tin, milk, ice, salt, song of
    common nouns.
Song of islands, gulls and a hawk high up, song of black water.
Song of the continuance, song of the ongoing.
Song of flagpoles and quarried granite, song of memorial stones,
    song of federal marble.
Song of arches, of flight and suspension, song of the bike path
    across the brook, fingering water sluiced and leapt over.
Song of channels, horizons, a bridge in the distance, song of the
    circle of distances.

· · · ·

Theme and variation, theme and variation.
Click-clack, click-clack:
hum, buzz, trill.

· · · ·

In this town the basketball courts are empty,
the crop in the field is houses,
the water tower has been spray painted: HI PIGS.

····

Three pumpkins on a back porch. Trestles
of an overpass
resembling Mandarin calligraphy.

Sparrows on a fence:
blurred cinders taking wing.

ADAM AND EVE

From the imperium, eyeless, tongueless,
to witness, to taste . . . . From the uranium cradle to hear
hosannas ascend from the ashes of rung bells . . . .

"(Sittin' on) The Dock of the Bay" is everywhere that year,
humming from the radio of the old blue Chevy
at the brand-new drive thru bank off Metzerot Road where

you'd get a purple lollipop from the lady if you were lucky.
And then Otis Redding died in the plane wreck,
or he already had, and that knowledge is bared to a child's scrutiny,

and the keen of it enhances the soundtrack,
grief and joy, each a movement, each a groove, each
a tone to be borne and abided, rueful and honey-struck

as the untroubled melancholy of his voice.
And then the assassination of Martin Luther King,
first glimmer of the ways in which

the melody's ampersand ensnares us, first inkling
of the intertwined harmony of self and society,
call and response, part and counterpart sung

in the choral grandiloquence of the common polity
while the grave robbers torching oblivion
comment more eloquently than any thin-tied anchor on TV,

my father's commute to the city dogged by the contagion
of Georgia Avenue storefronts looted to cinders.
And then my best friend's father sent off to Viet Nam—

we were still, marginally, military; Sunday dinner
at the Officers' Club—and the inverse celebration
when my uncle Billy pulled a lucky draft number.

He was my favorite babysitter, ball player, the one
who took me to the drive-in to see
the double-feature that poured a mythological foundation

for my adolescence—*The Good, the Bad, and the Ugly*,
followed by *One Million Years B.C.*
Clint Eastwood and Raquel Welch as Adam and Eve,

ideal gender models, everything we desired and desired to be.
How could I have known the years it takes to unlearn
certain lessons, singing "Sugar, Sugar" with the Archies

in the backseat while the honeycomb of our innocence burned
in the streets, everything we would inherit
cast and scorified in the crucible of those years?

How could I tell what was real from what was not?
When Raquel pawed her caveman I smiled,
when Clint said draw I shot.

ZEUGMA

Zeugma. From the Greek, *zeugnynai,* to join together; from
          a pair of animals linked at labor;
yoked oxen. The Greeks, of course, for whom beginnings signified
          better than endings, alpha & omega, for whom
x was just another letter: xiphoid, xerophagy, xenophobia, xoanon.
          Civilization, perforce, is abecedarian.
When Xenophon's hoplites charged the Persians at Cunaxa he
          denied the agency of local gods, mistaking
vox populi for *vox angelica,* voice of a suffering populace
          entirely freed of fleshly yoke,
uplifted in exquisite agony. Such are the costs of our transmigration.
          Fish demand ladders, wooden horses
transhumance, referring to reindeer but apropos in Ilium,
          green-fingered Lydia or Mesopotamia,
stage for the tidal clash of cultures & languages, ebbs & floods
          hardly unique to Persians & Greeks.
Recall the illiterate Pizarro against the hummingbird-feathered
          Inca Atahualpa, sun-god & moon-
queen trampled into Andean dust by a few dozen Spaniards
          jointly with their horses, gunpowder, &
priestly blessing to sanctify such slaughter in the name of the king of
          kings. Back to Xenophon & the Ten Thousand:
on the retreat now, following the Tigris, they come to a ruined city,
          Larissa, inhabited by Medes, thought to be

none other than Nimrud, ancient Kalhu, hippogriffs become
          Medean in the wake of serial conquest,
median point on their march from Babylon toward the hills of
     Armenia,
               none cheered by that barren vision, dire
Larissa, omen of defeat, citadel of political impermanence.
          On the next day, great Nineveh, abandoned:
kings, seneschals, satraps, jesters, fletchers, peltasts, potters,
          priestly & noble classes—vanished con-
jointly into equitable oblivion, weaver & wool, smith & tool,
          queen & fool. So much for the Assyrians.
Ink, a luxury, so no texts but wind-scoured stone remain to help us
          recall them, our contemporary ignorance
hardly less monumental than Xenophon's self-serving chronicle,
          scene by scene inventing ancient history.
Green no longer, that Fertile Crescent, mislabeled by an en-
          tranced human stab at metaphoric order.
Fish into amphibians, logograms into syllabaries, seas into lands
          uplifted in autochthonic agons
entirely unwitnessed, template free of cartographic correlatives,
          vox barbara or *vox nihilim*, celestial music
denied in our fury to claim an alphabet forged from the metals of
     chaos.
          When the ox moves, the plow moves.

Civilization, perforce, is boustrophedonic: *x-y-z; z-y-*
       x. Better the blue mud of the Euphrates,
better the raw ore of belief than these chains of syntax, this
       yoke of definitions. Xoanon:
a primitive idol resembling the rough block from which it was carved.
       Zeugma: maker & vessel, master & slave.

INFINITE NEEDS

But then, it was not until culture neared the height of its material achievements that it erected a shrine to the Unattainable: Infinite Needs.

—MARSHALL SAHLINS, "The Original Affluent Society"

I.

America's hunger takes nothing for granted.
Ants hollowing fallen fruit,
recasting the temple of the pomegranate,

mice in their congress of grain, squirrels in the heart
of a deciduous continental democracy,
mountains scored by rivulets,

granite beds, plains of salt or river clay,
subduction and production and consumption
driven by the master narrative of orogeny,

magma become lava in the instant of eruption
as a chocolate egg ruptures its shell of golden foil
in a hand that might belong to young Tom Jefferson

pursuing the butterfly of his happiness, or
Benjamin Franklin flying a kite,
or the daydreaming machinist Henry Ford

inventing the mass-market,
or you, or me, or everyone, or no one.
America's epic is the odyssey of appetite.

2.

After Laramie, the bad scene in Motel 6,
they follow the red lights of transcontinental rigs
across Wyoming in thickening weather,
through the Wasatch where a dozen splayed elk
hit by a truck at the false lick of rock salt
bleed the fast lane to ruddy ice, then skid
the last exit to escape an impending whiteout
in Salt Lake. In the morning they find
themselves snow-blind and heartsick
and the desert is a highway slick with frost
followed west to a world whose beauty
admonishes their tribulations,
their final night amid the mirrored walls
of the "adult motel" by the Oakland airport
all they can afford before her flight out
at dawn. When she leaves he wanders
San Francisco with a busted Walkman
and an old green sweater so full of holes
the waiter at a Chinese restaurant
sews them closed and slips the talisman
of a single tangled thread into his palm.

He heads north, hitchhiking I-5,
following two-lanes among orchards
into foothills scented with alkali dust.
Works for a while bottling cherry cider
beneath Mt. Shasta, works pumping gas
watching flocks of birds circle the buttes
and desolate lakes near Burns, Oregon,
eating cold hot dogs from the package,
hearing the tintinnabulation of his loneliness
in the chimings of a mouse
leaping from hanger to empty hanger
in the closet of the weed-fringed trailer.
Small friend, tiny bell ringer,
little comrade of the sunrise.
Spring, he follows the snowmelt rivers
coastward, sleeps among rosebushes
balled for replanting in Portland,
works cleaning floors at the aquarium,
works pulling racks from the oven
at Winchell's Donuts before dawn.
South to Coos Bay, the Lost Coast,
a meadow of salt hay in Albion.
Works the artichoke fields, quits, moves on.
Sleeps for weeks beneath a pier
near Monterey where, one night,
he alters form and swims the cold Pacific
as a sea lion, a transformation

that will prove impossible to explain
or comprehend through all the years
he carries the image of the kelp forest
engraved in his memory, inked
gravity of its groves and alcoves,
pods and tendrils, swirled hawsers
emerging in dream-time as a thread
through passages of abandoned shells
to the chamber of the Minotaur
like tarnished silver in the moonlight.
So Theseus was right, then,
having found himself in the maze,
in the vaulted death-stench of the bull,
to leave the black sails billowing.
There could be no return to his former life.
The labyrinth would live forever
within him, and he in it, waiting.

3.

The universe is a fire in which all things perish.
Every gem, every atom, every hyacinth
is consumed by the conflagration of time.

We dare not tarry in the ash fields
and we cannot halt the flames,

against which our hungers shine palely,
like mushrooms at the edge of a burning forest.

So we walk forth, into the future,
consuming as we are consumed.

WOE

Consider the human capacity for suffering,
our insatiable appetite for woe.
I do not say this lightly
but the sandwiches at Subway
suck. Foaming lettuce,
mayo like rancid bear grease,
meat the color of a dead dog's tongue.
Yet they are consumed
by the millions
and by the tens of millions.
So much for the food. The rest
I must pass over in silence.

ROCK AND ROLL

Been a long time since I rock & rolled
Led Zeppelin says in its famous song called,
quite rightly, "Rock and Roll,"

as so many are, so far so good,
but then what? *Been a long time since I did the stroll,*
as Robert Plant would have it understood,

or *been a long time since the Dead Sea Scrolls?*
Both, in their way, are intelligible,
both possess sense-making apparatus and obey syntactical protocols,

both signify, both are full
of meaning,
both call to us across the void—*hell-*

o!—but their ways and means
of meaning what they mean and saying what they say are as different
as night from day, the first a formulaic, stripped-clean,

boogie-woogie rant,
the second an implicit commentary on the historicity of the text,
a not uncommon species of lit-crit cant,

coy reference to the complexity
of deciphering what we hear and what we read
in or out of context,

like the time in Verona we could have seen Lou Reed
in the Roman amphitheater that is one of the glories of Western
     civilization
but Elizabeth wouldn't go because she thought I meant Lou Rawls.

HITS OF THE 70S

Can you hear the drums, Fernando?

At fourteen, George Washington is alone in the wilderness,
surveying the western districts for settlement,
but I'm still listening to Steely Dan,
contemplating virtuosity. How good is good
enough? How much polish is too much, how much
silver-toned studio gloss before the baby goes blind,
how much nectar, and of what bloom—
Can't Buy a Thrill—that ambrosia, that attar—
or *Aja* like some kind of holy cloud descending,
music in the blur-zone, V-necked leather with glissando,
skate the magic vibe and trill of marimba machinations,
zither and shimmer, shimmy and shake,
ride the cocaine snake to the neon North Hollywood
studio of chromium acoustics and sonic acrostics,
little night flower of my heart gone to seed in the shade
of such arbors of blossoming oleander. Shh,
the sheaf of silent ears falls slyly. Hush, sugar. Hush.
And was it three or only two summers later
the slate-roofs of Paris confided the intricacies of their art
as I walked the streets of the Latin Quarter
fueling the arson of my first broken heart with *vin
ordinaire* and apple-bongs of Moroccan hash
and the kerosene catechism of "Prove It All Night"?
Baby, tie your hair back in a long white bow,

meet me in the fields behind the dynamo.
Back at the hostel we touched burning matches to the sheets
from sheer anomie; our palms ached with flame
and our spines lit up like reliquary miracles.
What was it all about, this thing between women and men?
What did it mean, what was it worth, and anyway,
what was a dynamo? Was it Paris? Springsteen?
Was I the dynamo, whirling within my dog's-night of desolation,
mawkishly sentimental as the harpsichord chorale
we drank gin to in the last pew of some candlelit cathedral?
And how many more years until I arrive in Berlin
on yet another overcrowded European sleeper, teeth blued
from the lees of a life Shane MacGowan might envy,
alone at dawn with the street sweepers in the zoo
eating day-old bread and drinking Soviet vodka
while the weirdly militaristic animals
box and gore and claw each other to pieces?
So let's not glamorize loneliness and dazed exhaustion,
please. Let's remember the dead rats in the futon
on Columbus Avenue, the lost music of sunrise,
the smell of tar and Benzedrine and rain.
Or must we privilege public discourse over private grief,
generational anthems that articulate the zeitgeist,
protest ballads, love songs that recall a particular summer,
taste of Coppertone and August grass heavy on our tongues,
the Raspberries urging us to "Go All the Way,"

"O What a Night," Frampton—the talking guitar!—please
don't even begin to suggest that "Show Me the Way"
does not contain some pith or core immeasurable to man,
a pearl of priceless worth in its innocence.
In 1976 the issue of foremost world-historical import
was the power and pathos of *Born to Run,*
which side of the album was better, which song definitive—
"Thunder Road," or "Jungleland," or "Backstreets"—
so went the days and nights at Camp Shohola, anyway,
scratching the same stale groove on the beat-up record player
that spoke to our status as "Counselors in Training."
Only one guy in the cabin claimed not to care,
whose face I've forgotten but whose nickname was Sarge
and who wanted, inexplicably, to become either an accountant
or a comic book illustrator when we "grew up,"
and who demanded equal airplay for his Aerosmith and Kiss
and god knows what else—the Nuge!—and so
we endured "Calling Dr. Love" and "Big Ten Inch Record"
and the shrill caterwaul of "Cat Scratch Fever"
until, over time, we came to like them too.
Came, almost, to love them. Perhaps
we would have grown to like anything eventually, no matter
its pubescent vulgarity, no matter the reductivism of its rant.
But no, there were limits even to our debasement:
not Elton John nor Abba nor the Captain and Tennille,
none of the androgynous stars of the Top 40

from whom we insistently distanced ourselves.
It was all wrapped up with our own un-
certain sexual identities, I can see now, giddy lust-howls
to hot-cocked love guns and chrome-tuned engines,
girls objectified to inscrutable enigmas
or etherealized to subjects of smirking gratification
until we slept with cheerleaders in the backseats of cars
or honor students in lacustrine meadows
or both or neither and it no longer mattered
once the Ramones arrived at rock and roll high school
and we burned our Boston records, ripped holes in our jeans,
pogoed and slam danced and lay around dazed
and confused on Coco Lopez and Wild Irish Rose
and sheer infatuation at our own hip insouciance.
Looking back I'm struck by the gentility of our revolt,
by how naïve and credulous I must have been
to believe the Sex Pistols when they said *We mean it, man,*
and while being sixteen most certainly influenced
my "decision-making process" I'm still inclined
to lay some portion of the blame at society's feet,
not like screaming down the alley with a bloody switchblade
"It's society's fault I killed Ricky, man," not that,
not a criminal indictment but a class-action proceeding
against the rampant idiocy and bewildering tastelessness
of a cultural moment when the late-night streets fielded rival clans
of mohawked punks and Deadheads and Rocky Horror devotees
while we just wanted to sneak into bars, throw ashtrays at the stage,

listen to Tex Rubinowitz and the Bad Boys play rockabilly,
and beg free drinks during the break. To beg, that is,
ironically. "Ironically." Irony was our uniform,
our master trope, our jungle gym, our saucer-lid of potato agar,
the mechanism that transformed the twin currents
of our ambivalence into negotiable currency,
a dual-track recorder on which to create the stereophonic tape-loop
played like a subliminal soundtrack in 70 mm Sensurround
to explicate the dailies of the real-time disaster movie
we found ourselves acting bit parts in.
Irony was our baptismal font, our Lethe and our Styx,
a good scrubbing with a cake of Irish Spring soap
and afterward a golden-haired girl in Shetland wool
to hand us a towel and coo, "Manly, yes, but I like it too!"
Which was cool and also not so cool. Which was
amazing, banal, grave, risible, gleefully schizophrenic
as was so much of the hothouse-potlatch-sweet-potato-patch
in which we were seeded and weeded and bedded and pruned
by the green-thumbed programmers and market mavens
and demented social visionaries of Madison Avenue
creating the commodified, media-driven culture of consumption
which was even more uniquely a consumable culture,
whose very flesh provided a paradoxical, Froot Loopian
awakening to the mechanisms of the marketplace,
a fetishized, sucrotic, quasi–*Soylent Green* enlightenment.
To them it was data arbitrage and blunt demographics,
while we, who were its children, for whom the culture led, first,

the antic, disposable, damsel-fly life span envisioned by the
    theocracy,
and second a furtive, larval, hierophantic existence
within the very cells of its cannibalistic offspring,
we, at least, grasped and acknowledged the studied hypocrisy
and cynical propagandistic dualism of it all:
hate is love and hope is despair and death is beauty,
we must win the war, we must sell more cereal,
what's good for General Motors is good for General Mills,
there will be starvation and there will be toaster pastries—
caution: do not leave toaster unattended; caution:
fruit filling may cause burns if hot—whatever, you fools,
you simpletons, you ants, you zombies
in your dreary, disciplined, ritualized conformity.
Fuck you! Your music sucks! We mean it, man!
But, in the end, we didn't. Not really.
Or, we meant it more than Johnny Rotten
but less deeply than our rhetoric implied. Or maybe
we really did mean it and just outgrew the need
to broadcast the sincerity of our cynicism
as we slipped ever deeper into the law-and-order 80s,
a decade which served as a tough-love boot camp
to which the dysfunctional 70s were sent to sober up.
During Operation Desert Storm the very first song
broadcast over Armed Forces Radio was "Rock the Casbah,"
certainly an ironic act of appropriation given the pretensions
of the Clash, but which, more importantly, I remember

ad-libbing drunk and out of control to a pissed-off crowd
the very week that album was first released,
our band already zeroed-in to its inexorable decline,
glorious only in our own minds, nothing in the world
to match that 3 a.m. sensation that the party's over
and they wish you'd pack up the amps and leave
but you're working seven unmitigated minutes of noise
across the ceiling as if the golden host were every bit localized
up in those rafters or tiles or branches or rooftops,
up in the hammers and diamonds and smoke,
meaningless fretwork arabesques tossed
like handfuls of precious figs to the faithful air,
to the last fans and party stalwarts stacked
like a sticky lumpenproletariat against the bar.
What a high, that energy, the memory of that edge,
the chaos of performance or for that matter practice
in someone's Dad's garage or faux-"Bonanza" rec room,
high hat, chicken scratch, bassline, feedback,
speed and power, grace and frenzy, the esthetic dialectic
of Orphic lyricism and Dionysian excess,
though for that matter the rank vapidity of corporate
candyland gloss-and-schlock held its own appeal,
and come to think of it, that same gig we played,
along with our cherished originals and standard Ramones covers,
a Ted Nugent song—"White Buffalo"—and Kiss, too—
"Rock and Roll All Night (And Party Every Day),"
and whatever else drifted into our heads, "Night Moves"

and "Wildfire" and "Shadow Play" and "Sweet Jane"
and Wire and the DeFranco Family and Blue Öyster Cult
and Heart and Bread and Kansas and America and
that song by Toto, "Africa," that could serve as poster child
for witlessness and poverty of imagination.
By then it was all over, the 70s were history, charred toast,
and few even now would champion them, or wish them back,
and their music endures mainly as hum-along nostalgia
or jingles for bagmen by whom we have been targeted
for the purchase of new automobiles and skin cologne,
but what I really want to know, what I need to know,
now, and still, for closure, is what they were saying
in that song—*I'd miss the rains down in Africa*
or *God Bless the waves down in Africa* or something
in between? And what might either version mean?
And what wild and generous deity allows such candles
to burn on her altar and condones this reverence
for the fragments of a past as illusory as it is absurd?
Yes, of course, I know: the girl with the blue plastic radio.

THE MAELSTROM

Chicago, 1980: heroic journey of the all-night viewer
in the pre-cable, three-network, UHF era;
a labor of love to outlast Johnny Carson and Tom Snyder,

and then the real work, the long haul, beyond *Baretta,*
beyond Jack Lord, beyond Jim and Tammy Faye praising the lord,
beyond the *Late, Late Movie* starring Tony Franciosa

to the small deep hours of illuminated boredom,
F Troop and *Voyage to the Bottom of the Sea,*
dismal reruns from an almost-forgotten hoard,

bottom of the whirlpool of sleeplessness and bad coffee,
vortex of images in a ruined theater the culture comes to resemble,
if only one could extricate oneself in the half-light, work free

of the rubble or cry for help, like the little girl who fell
in the oil well or the old hole in the cornfield in the dark
with everyone watching a live feed except this well

is the ravening whirlpool of America
itself, the one with the red-lettered emergency exits to hell,
the one amid the floes and skellings of the Arctic

in the book I read a hundred childhood nights in thrall
to Jules Verne and Edgar Allen Poe, almanac of wonders
engraved with the Maelstrom's tidal whirl,

ineluctable and super cool, as years later
certain music came to sound on the Wildcat record player,
form inventing itself from the rough notes of matter,

music like the heaving of giant boulders in elder days,
music that casts burnt figures against infinity,
coalescing in laminate layers

like a galaxy flattened to the disc of its destiny,
gripped by the unseen, shaped and devoured,
possessed of dark gravity,

mineral-rich, dense and unforged, pure ore.
And then: sign off. 4 a.m. Hour of uneasy vigil,
hour of fear and clarity, liminal hour

of solitude before the electronic hearth is rekindled,
bright burning campfire of the TV
lit by the pre-dawn farm report, by Rocky & Bullwinkle.

Out the window: ghastly fluorescence of the 24-hour A&P,
welfare mothers buying pork chops and margarine,
economy sacks of frozen black-eyed peas;

silver chain of ice along the lake like a charm
bracelet strung with netless basketball hoops; the urge
the water feels to carve the granite blocks to more organic form—

Henry Moore, brass rebus of sublimated rage,
his sculpture by the library to fix
and sanctify the birthplace of the Atomic Age.

Sign off: Blue Angels rampant on a field of static,
anthem and flag descending to darkness.
And the snow's immaculate fallout, its slick

erasure, its test-pattern hiss.
And the will to endure the winter.
And the vow to give voice to that silence.

XENA, WARRIOR PRINCESS

Absolutely everyone is wild about
Buffy, the Vampire Slayer, and hey, why not?
Cute as a little blonde button, no
doubt. It's just that I'm more
easily excited by chicks in bondage straps and chain mail jerkins,
forgive me, it happens that I dig Xena's thing, I
go ballistic when she and Hercules
hook up, oh man,
it's incredible what that's like. Pure gravy. 100% natural
juice. I'm cranked just thinking about Xena
killing all the extras in a flourish after the third commercial.
Listen, it's not as totally screwed up as it sounds.
My ancient TV gets, like, 60-something channels.
No way is that full spectrum, I mean, it's
opening another can of nuts altogether but how can I be
positive there's not some even more red-blooded
queen of ambidextrous rubber swordplay out there, some
righteous cable access babe in skin-tight
skins or tights, or neanderthal whatnot, or silver
Teflon space bikini, or that black elastic rattlesnake suit
Uma wore in *The Avengers,* Uma, the uber-
vixen. But what a movie—
woof! Some are born to run and some are born to rerun,
Xena, so let's ride into that sunset together, babe,
you with a posse of buffed-up gal pals, me at my
Zenith of carnage and woo.

LOVE©

I've got the copyright on love, honey baby.
Registered patent number such &

such. Don't dillydally with saxifrage
& sassafras, don't bother me with this & that,

don't mix the salt in my vanilla. You think
a bird in the eye of the ocean of springtime

knows love? Cinnamon, I'm drowning in it.
Don't tell me it's cold because I'm burning

with it. I've got the trademark, I've got the copyright,
cupcake, sweet molasses, sugar pie.

IOWA

First trip alone across the country: a dream of driving
through driving rain in Iowa, sodden Iowa,
miles of drenched earth passed through in the gloaming,

roads of pickup trucks, hog pens, cornbins, silos,
a grocery where I stop for apples and white bread,
streetlights reflected on asphalt and dented iron,

on a bright orange Subaru I acknowledge with a nod
as I acknowledge myself, behind the wheel,
Woody Guthrie and the Ramones, the open road,

all that, the scope of the world, its gravity and zeal
beyond rain-wet windows, its diverse
and circumstantial passage, even the familiar become unreal

in light of that unscrolling: taste of liverwurst
and sweet pickle sandwiches; tears of a woman
on a pay phone beside a piebald horse

in some city flashing past, gone,
perhaps Cedar Rapids; atavistic vision of deepest greenness,
the summoning sheen and wavelength of the corn,

as if the kernels radiated an oceanic luminescence
the husks worked to cocoon and sequester
back into the dark. Of course it was

all much stranger than that, richer and sadder
in its unique and particular word-defying actuality
than my familiar penciled grid of sequential semesters.

Different how, in what way? I can't say.
I mean that it is unsayable, a string of precious shells
or trading beads—*cow, brook, hay*—

not the coinage of names but the things themselves,
their totality, their scale and dimension,
the knowledge that there are spheres and levels

one has never conceived: so this is what the rain
feels like in Iowa, in California; this is another way,
another state, another life, another vision.

And then what? What to equal that revelatory awe?
Elizabeth's beauty like an exhibition
of blown-glass roses, her heart's raw glory,

the birth of our children,
that great awakening, leaving the hospital
our first morning together like a vestal procession

passing from the lobby into the lightfall
of a pure blue Chicago spring
as if crossing some threshold of universal

import, powered by mysterious agency, a door opening
silently as the future opens its automatic portal
before us, second by second, invisible and astonishing.

My son is born and I am no longer immortal.
The ring shall be closed, the cycle fulfilled.
I am bound over, as in a fairy tale,

to the will of time, pledged to this world
by an oath of fearful enchantment.
Pledged. Promised. Bound over. Beguiled.

OF PURE FORMS

Anatomy, as Da Vinci saw it; the human
body as godly investiture;
clavicle and scapula, travertine and chalcedony.

*

Desire vs. lust; X-rays vs. klieg lights.

*

Eggs as a modality, as an ergonomic method or a model economy.
Fields become a sea of grass in wind across certain
Great Plains states, i.e., South Dakota.

*

Hearing the chirping of tree frogs, you think: *crickets*.
It answers: *night spirits*.

*

Jellyfish oblivious to the shadow of the shark.
Kentucky, as Daniel Boone saw it.
Luna moths, lunar modules, the lunatic fringe.

*

Many in the guise of one.
None,
or none other than what was. The ex-nihilo. The
pre-extant.

*

Quartz, quicksilver, the quavering of temple bells.
Radishes: the way they spray and bag and stack them at the
       produce market, like sacks of rough terra-cotta marbles.
Sodium pentathol.
The giant ants in *Them*; Clint Eastwood in *High Plains Drifter*.
Ur, city of chalk and papyrus.

*

Vessels of fresh oil; orchards on the terraces above Paleokastritsa;
       hemlock, live oak, kumquat, cedar—
whatever species of trees are still inhabited by dryads.

*

X for what it is; x as x.
Yellow shutters on a house of weathered shingles among sand dunes.
Zinc, humblest of metals.

JACK GILBERT

Take a hammer to an amphora of blue Euphrates clay
and it will fracture meticulously there, and there,
and there, the way a sentence yields at the invisible
seams and faults of grammar's fluid syntactical
tectonics. Take a chisel to the mountainside—basalt,
gabbro, porphyry—and, well, what did you expect?

JEFFREY LEE PIERCE

Jeffrey Lee Pierce is dead, at age 37, in Salt Lake City, Utah.

R.I.P., J.L.P.

What tenuous clichés, the unrusted corpse and the early grave, stupidly traditional rock and roll icons, though he was anything but a traditionalist, and so it rang as a double surprise, coming across his obit in the *Times*—that he was gone, yes, prematurely and forlornly; and that they had deemed his passing worthy of notice, esteemed him an artist of such cultural significance, because I really hadn't known there were that many others out there listening, that many who valued his music as I did, took him seriously, saw him play half a dozen times across the years, the many permutations of the Gun Club behind him, early '80s blues-punks and middle-era noise mongers and the elegant, rawboned, in-exile band, but always the same old Jeffrey Lee, spaghetti epic in a Fassbinder overcoat singing "Ghost on the Highway" and "She's Like Heroin to Me" with the atonal wail of a leopard-skin banshee, a bleached-blond voodoo doll of Elvis circa *Flaming Star* spraying gunslinger guitar solos to the western wind, sawed-off and smacked-out, smiling at the crowd with hip condescension informed by self-awareness, or so I always felt, such was the image I had composed of him, though it may be he was just a junkie-with-an-attitude nobody much cared for, as they say in the rock and roll "press," I have no evidence to the contrary but the testimony of my ears, and I'm not suggesting he was any kind of genius, but I do think he was good at what he did.

And the more I learn about anything

the more I respect that: being good; skill, craft, knowledge of form;

after which comes passion, commitment, belief in the ideal, faith in the power of noise to transcend the graffitied walls of this cinder block sub-basement rock club of a world;

which is art;

which resides in the eye of the beholder.

So have I bent to the grace notes and troubling invective of his music, a dark embryo hungry for oxygen, an unfinished chrysalis of ecstatic rage. So have I hunched to listen, in the small hours, as for a benediction or sonic transcendence, trill of some message expertly encrypted. Did I find it? No. But then, I didn't really expect to. Not yet. Maybe never, now that Jeffrey Lee is dead, though I am only one of many still listening, at least I have learned that much now, one of many bound to bear witness to what lives on long after the voice of the singer has gone.

A song.

There. Can you hear it?

GUNS N' ROSES

i.m. Tim Dwight, 1958–1994

Not a mea culpa, not an apology, but an admission:
there are three minutes in the middle of "Sweet Child o' Mine"
that still, for all the chopped cotton of the passing years,
for all the muddled victories and defeats of a lifetime,
for all the grief and madness and idiocy of our days,
slay me, just slay me. They sound like how it felt to be alive
at that instant, how it was to walk the streets of Manhattan
in that era of caviar and kill-hungry feedback,
the Big Apple so candy-coated with moral slush and easy money
even the corporate heavyweights could fashion no defense
against decay, all the homeless encamped over cold coffee
at Dunkin' Donuts on upper Broadway, even McDonald's
become a refugee camp for victims of the unacknowledged war
fought beneath the giddy banners of corporatization
as the decade spun down its drain of self-delusion. *Where
do we go, where do we go, where do we go
now?* What a glorious passage, a shimmering bridge
embodying everything rock and roll aspires to be,
heroic and violent and joyous and juvenile
and throbbing with self-importance and percolating
with melodrama and thrilled and scared by
its own anthemic power, by the kid-on-a-scooter freedom
and the hill a lot steeper than it seemed at first glance,
what the hell, rust never sleeps, live and let die, etc., etc.
And whenever I hear that song, become, now,
a classic of the genre, even as it suffuses me with nostalgia
for those days of malt liquor and bbq chips,

it gives me cause to think of Axl Rose in his purgatory
self-assembled from paranoia and Malibu chaparral,
wrestling exotic demons, kickboxing with Jesus,
binding and gagging his women with duct tape in the closet,
much the way the heavy metal mentality of the times
seized and militarized his music, sonic warriors
blasting "Paradise City" at the Panamanian dictator,
"Welcome to the Jungle" for the Waco cultists,
Slash and Axl circling the globe, leveling ancient civilizations
with power chords and teenage emotions,
from the Halls of Mentholyptus to the Shores of MTV.
And if Axl appears almost Nixonian in his anguish,
at least he is not Kurt Cobain, forsaken and baby-faced
as J. Michael Pollard in the episode of *Lost in Space*
where Penny goes through the mirror to a realm
of demoniacal toys and that metaphysical bear-monster,
cousin to the troglodytes that chased Raquel Welch
up the cavern tree in *One Million Years B.C.*,
death in its many B-movie guises, so much gaudier
than the killers that walked the streets among us,
the needle and the dollar, the gun and the rose,
and the last time we saw Tim, at Bruce's place
in the Hollywood hills, he recalled the first time
we'd all hung out together in New York, Halloween, 1985,
provincial immigrants tossing back bourbon and tequila,
Tim holding a bundle of Ecstasy for some dealer—
a drug I'd never even heard of—which instead of trying to market

he handed around with cavalier generosity,
packets of powder doused in the tall cans of Colt 45
we drank as we walked the streets of the Village
amidst the disintegrating drifts and dregs of the parade,
and finally a midnight show at the Ritz, some L.A. bands
the girls adored done up in black-light fluorescents,
dancing and stage-diving, jubilant and hallucinatory,
getting home somehow on a subway serviced
by orange-vested trolls before waking to cold sweat
and hangover candy and a day of recuperation and the desire
to do it all again. Because there was plenty of time,
we knew, or thought we knew, or were simply too stupid
not to know we didn't know at all, time to waste or kill
before the crashes and commitments that would doom or save
or cast us back into the tide pools of the westering continent.
Tim was still laughing, hauntingly frail, but what I thought
looking out across the canyon was how badly
Los Angeles had aged, wanton and care-worn,
like a faded child star sickled with cosmetic surgery scars
still dreaming of a comeback, still scheming and groveling,
as if to prove that nothing really dies in America
but is merely removed from the shelves for repackaging,
coming back crisper and crunchier, cholesterol-free,
as even Axl Rose is coming back with Tommy Stinson on bass
and a sideman wearing a KFC bucket like a Spartan helmet,
and I wish that I could lay the blame for Axl's fucked-up life
on the feral orphanhood of the Pax Atomica,

the alienation of lives begun with no expectation of completion,
it would be simpler that way, for all of us,
but the world did not end in a vortex of toxic fire,
the flying fortresses have returned from the stratosphere
and the missiles endure their nightmares mutely in dark silos
and we have no excuse but the arrogance of power for our narcissism
and no solace but the merciless amplitude of our din.
And that was it, the moment had passed,
another gem or tear for the cut-glass diadem of passing years.
Someone cranked the music up, someone made a toast
to the pool lights and glitter. And then the Pixies
begin some riff-rife, fully surfable rifle-shot of a theme song
announcing the ironic revival of our childhood
swaggering like Tony the Tiger atop a station wagon
at an Esso station in 1964, Tony the Tiger
back from the dead, eldritch and transcendent—
rise, the immortals!—
rise to grasp the silver handles
of the casket in procession before us, Ultraman
and Astroboy and Mr. Clean and the Man from Glad
and Josie & the Pussycats
on the Rose Bowl float with their God
Bless America batons a-twirl
and then—
huh—
cue the horns,
take it down, break it all apart

and start from nothing to garb our nakedness
with sheets of beaten gold,
cozen us with grieving blossoms,
anoint us with honey in the dry riverbed,
and tell me,
o great devourer,
o master of thorns and ashes,
where do we go
now?

HOME

Lived for a while in a mobile home
parked in the driveway of a house in Long Beach, California.
Typical development of bungalows and ranch homes,

split-level evidence of the post-war euphoria,
all the streets in the subdivision named for state capitals.
Lincoln, Bismarck, Providence, Olympia.

At 6:30 the dads come home in their blue sedans full
of mid-level-white-collar-aerospace anxiety
and plunk down on the couch to lull themselves civil

with vodka and reruns of *WKRP in Cincinnatti*.
The kids grow up surfing in the late imperial sunlight,
man the registers at Taco Bell and Hardee's,

attend Golden West Community College at night,
graduate to a career shilling car wax supplies, hooking up
pay phones, managing a franchise for Chicken Dee-Lite.

It was Dave's family's place, the house where he grew up.
The mobile home was called "The Dolphin."
There were other vehicles, many of them, cars and pickups,

motorcycles, a house like a shrine to material possessions—
but I don't intend to critique the social mores
of those whose ambient generosity I sheltered within.

How long did I live there? Am I certain anymore
of the circumstances of my exile, drawn west
as by magnetic force on a current of blue agave

toward a collective future foreshadowed in smog alerts,
HOV lanes, and "restaurant style" tortilla chips?
Days, Dave and I would bodysurf and housepaint,

then hit the local sawdust dives and happy hour spots;
nights we'd seek out music at Madame Wong's or the Whiskey,
or follow his brother to some hardcore thrashathon of the unhip

in the deepest recesses of Orange County,
mosh-pit frenzy of testosterone and alienation
as the metalhead kids and the skatepunk kids and the latchkey

legions without rhythmic allegiance or tribal affiliation
pogo and slam and already the riot cops aligned in helmeted array
in the lemon-scented air outside the auditorium—

California like the Roman Empire in its iron naïveté!—
and the black copter braceleted in searchlights
bellowing through its megaphone: *By order of the L.A.*

P.D.—disperse! A truly funny thought,
all that energy amped to a peak of inchoate expression
told simply to disappear, fly away, like winged seeds in the moonlight.

It was the usual telegram of blustering intimidation
for which the young are paged by the forces of social order—
their job was to deliver it: ours was to run—

the defining drama of civilization, diverting that river
of violent enthusiasm around the waterfall
and into a spillway of car wax supplies, the safe reservoir

of sales clerks at the Payless Shoesource in the strip mall.
Disperse! Disperse!
Not likely, not likely at all.

THE INFORMATION AGE

What they mean when they say we're living in
the Information Age
is the Olympian vox populi of CNN

as global witness to our local forms of carnage;
the axe-clash of data giants in quest of net worth;
emerging markets maxing the sweet-pea amperage

that fuels the rise of the Cartoon Network
in a realm of flesh-and-bone cartoons
whose Babel of thought-balloons no longer works

and a new millennium dawns:
a thousand years of Scooby-Doo,
a thousand years of oblivion.

THE GLANN ROAD

Artichoke and thistle: two purples.
Artichoke, thistle, salsify, clover, lavender, loosestrife.
Blue is another country, another realm or province,

blue is a fiefdom unknown to the bees who gang the beds of heather,
heads bowed and beaded in fealty to the Land of Nod.

Clouds are another story altogether,
clouds in their pilgrimage across that starry
demesne, another lifetime, future and past
erased like the rib-blue slate that
floors the lake in sheets as terse as syllables.

Gaillimh: curragh, longboat, hooker. A white horse in the meadow.

Hydrangea the color of melon rind; of indigo, oyster shell, guelder
rose.
Hydrangea in the meadow the color of mist, of the piebald mule
seeking shelter beneath the giant oak
islanded in an ocean of black wasps drunk on clover flower.
Joy of the nectar-sated, the smoke-holy,
Kevin in the sanctity of his cold-water tribulation
long before whomever it was
left these ruins of monastic simplicity
marooned amid the heath and ancient yews,
nave, bier, cist,

oracle or temple, scatter of fieldstone, crusheen like a transmitter
pulsing devotion, whatever energy that is, radiant as faith,
quasar or saturnic ring, the stolid earth, its moon,
rocks in a high and lonely place,
six round cobbles from the waters of Lough Corrib,
stones in their orphanhood, their antigravitational hegira,
their lithic ascension
toward fields of hagiographic light.

To locate the self without compass on a lake of many islands,
teal against alum, topaz on shale.

To defend the ancient tower from the piracy of the other, floribunda
          the color of sea-salt, fist of the artichoke cloaked in thistle.

To relent. To surrender to the hydrangea. To give oneself over
          to the blossoming tendrils of the sweet-pea vine,
their vellum prolixity
trellised against a hayrick of rain and a rainbow gone
underground. And the green snake,

vivid as myth, dreaming the spiral of a pre-Celtic divinity,

wild swans in a cove of reeds, a prayer to Saint Francis
Xavier, cerulean offerings to Elatha or Cernunnos,
yesterday's cuttings to propitiate a blue goddess:

zinnia, witches' thimble, chicory, forget-me-not.

TWO SONGS

1. NORTH CAROLINA

The more you allow the figures of black, silent trees glimpsed by night from the window of a train near Fayetteville into your heart, the greater the burden you must carry with you on your journey, and the sooner you will come to question your ability to endure it, and the stronger your conviction to sing.

2. TIGER

A tiger on our block, a real tiger, ivory and mallow orange, coiled and sinewed, caged in the back of a pickup truck in the driveway of the house of the two married models who live three doors down, for a fashion shoot. These things happen in Miami Beach. Beautiful, they are, beautiful animals. Six months later she leaves him. And the sound of his rock and roll band now, in the empty house, at all hours, practicing.

EVERYBODY KNOWS JOHN LENNON IS DEAD

Seated on the avenue eating almond ice cream beneath the orange trees
the Andalusian heat seems at last to have lessened, or
at least there is a breeze to squall the dusty citrus leaves

along the cobbled alleyways as a mélange of ambient music emerges
from the barrio—Eurodisco, Hendrix and the Beatles,
flamenco guitar. A kid on a Vespa hops the curb to deliver

a serrano ham to the bar across the street,
joint of a pig wrapped in muslin carried cross town
on his shoulder. Nice to know they still resist our microbial foibles,

our fetish with sterility, though there are clearly some
exotic new strains of growth in Sevilla's petrie dish.
You can tell how much has changed by the Germans begowned

in halter tops and spandex shorts milling in fiendish
prolixity around a Cathedral that resembles a reticulated spider
escaped from some dank cage of the Iberian Dark Age. As if

every least rain droplet of the future were not equally and altogether
new, alike as minted coins or the waters of the fountain before
    El Giralda
toward which even now the carriage horses stare in mute desire.

Strange the way one's life comes to seem a historical diorama,
looking back as from rocky peaks across golden valleys
where regiments of moonlit sunflowers lay siege to the Alhambra.

Sometimes, in the childhood of a now past century,
my family would forgo dinner to banquet on banana splits
at the old Gifford's ice cream parlor out the parkway,

with the ornate water fountain and marble tabletops,
cloth napkins and fluted silver spoons and formal glassware,
as here, though this, however reminiscent, is not

American ice cream. You can tell by the intensity of flavor,
the almondness of the almond, as you can tell from the woven rubber
chairs that this is not my long-gone suburbia, or any American
     anywhere,

though it could perhaps be Rome, thirty years ago, when the street
     vendors
hawked necklaces of hammered iron nails wired to leather thongs
and those clickety-clackety plastic bolas in the floodlights along the
     Tiber,

a city of bridges and diesel fumes and casual decay, like this one,
though you can tell it isn't Rome by the scent of rotten citrus in
    the air,
and the muzzled shadows of Moorish arches, and the wine is wrong,

and though it is always childhood for somebody, somewhere,
it certainly isn't mine—you can tell because the boys
are drawing aliens on the place mats with sugar-crystal hair,

still moving forward, not yet dreaming in reverse,
trafficking in a brotherhood that promises never to end,
and when "Strawberry Fields" fades down to street noise,

Jackson asks, *Which Beatle sings that one, Dad?*
And Sam says, *John Lennon.*
And Jackson says, *Idiot—everybody knows John Lennon is dead.*

ALSO BY CAMPBELL McGRATH

FLORIDA POEMS
ISBN 0-06-052736-6 (paperback)

Place-bound and tightly focused, McGrath's message is
nonetheless universal, as his penetrating vision
of Florida is also a vision of America.

"It is between the extremities of the exotic and the vulgar, and
of dread and hope, that this fierce book runs its course."
—*New York Times Book Review*

ROAD ATLAS
Prose and Other Poems
ISBN 0-06-093510-3 (paperback)

From Brazil to Manitoba, Las Vegas to Miami Beach,
McGrath charts a poetics of place and everyday experience.
Road Atlas is personal, provocative, and accessible—
the finest work yet from "the most Swiftian poet of his
generation" (David Biespiel, *Hungry Mind Review*).

SPRING COMES TO CHICAGO
ISBN 0-880-01484-9 (paperback)

McGrath pushes deeper into the jungle of American culture,
exposing and celebrating our native hungers and dreams.
Whether viewing this life with existential gravity or
consumerist glee, this is poetry that is at once
public and profoundly personal.

AMERICAN NOISE
ISBN 0-880-01374-5 (paperback)

"Campbell McGrath writes big, roughhousing, tender,
visionary, reckless, purely American poems. He's a passionate
democrat, the Whitman of our spoiled world. This is a
brilliant, disturbing book." —Chase Twichell

Visit www.AuthorTracker.com
for exclusive updates on your favorite authors.

Available wherever books are sold, or call 1-800-331-3761 to order.

www.HarperCollins.com/Ecco
ecco